Welcome to my recipe book, I hope you enjoy trying out my tasty meals and snacks on your journey to a healthier you.

Jx

Contents

Eating to Achieve

Eating to Achieve

Putting the right fuel into your body is so important and this book is not about depriving and punishing your body in order to lose fat. It is about nourishing it and providing your body with the best nutrients to reach your goals.
Along with achieving fat loss from eating well, your body starts to run like a well-oiled machine; things such as having more energy, radiant skin, glossy hair and feeling more confident about your image, are all things you'll start to notice.
In this section about fuelling your body, you'll get the low down on how to get the most from your meals, fit them into your busy lifestyle and develop a healthy relationship with some wonderful foods.

Our ingredients...who stays ...who goes!?

During your journey through my book, you'll be trying new foods and hopefully ditching some of those naughty ones that will stand in the way of achieving the most from your body.

Sugar

Unfortunately, a lot of us have a sweet tooth, and the problem with that, is that sugar doesn't provide us with anything useful!

There are so many hidden sugars in the foods we find on the supermarket shelves it is often hard to avoid them. In this book I provide some delicious recipes using unrefined sugars to keep the sweet tooth at bay but providing a healthier alternative.

When we consume sugar, it triggers the release of insulin into the bloodstream to remove the sugar; this is then stored as fat, a lot of this around the waist... not helpful! Sugar also affects the absorption of vitamins and minerals, meaning that the body is deprived of the goodness that helps you to look and feel great! Because your body lacks these vitamins and minerals, it is also hungry for them, meaning it wants you to eat more and more to try and feed this hunger for vital V&Ms...ironically, overweight people are often malnourished due to eating too much, of the wrong stuff!!

How do we avoid sugar?

When we think sugar, we think biscuits, chocolate bars and cake! But it is hidden in so many other foods, many you wouldn't suspect!

o Low fat or 'diet' products (yes they may be low in fat, but to make them taste of something sugar is added!)

o Bread (try making your own using one of my recipes, then you know exactly what's in there!)

o Breakfast Cereals (so many cereals are coated in or contain a lot of sugar, even the misleading 'healthy looking' granola, why not try making your own?

Fat

Everyone hears the word fat and shudders, eating fat makes you fat right? .... Wrong!
Fat is an essential nutrient required by the body for many every day functions including keeping the nervous system functioning well, good for concentration, good for the immune system and absorbing essential vitamins. It is also an energy source and make your food taste yummy!

When I refer to fat, I mean good fats, the stuff found in nuts, seeds, fish, dairy and meat. Not that found in pastry and processed foods; these bad fats are those that have been hydrogenated and become a 'trans fat'. These trans fats are heavily linked to conditions such as high levels of bad cholesterol, diabetes, obesity and cancer.

So it's best to avoid these if possible!

o Margarine products (switch for butter)
o Take away foods
o Shop bought pastry and pies
o Manufactured cakes and biscuits

And look for these to use in your kitchen instead...

o **Coconut oil**- this acts as an antiviral and anti-microbial agent and can't turn into a trans-fat when heated, it can also help with fat burning by increasing your energy expenditure.
o **Avocados** – these go well with so many other different foods and are great for the hair, skin and nails
o **Nuts and seeds** – these contain a range of vitamins and minerals and are a tasty little snack or ingredient for an exciting dish!
o **Goats cheese, halloumi, yoghurt & dairy in general**- these are tasty ingredients but try not to overload on the fats from dairy as you can soon consume a lot of calories. I like to eat a lot of natural yoghurt but to keep calories down I do have the 0% fat as this is still a good source of protein. I make sure there are no other added ingredients though, so I'm not getting any extra sugar or other nasty ingredients.
o **Fish rich in omega 3 (such as salmon)** are linked to so many health benefits including good heart health.

Protein

Many people associate protein with body builders, but the human body actually requires protein to function properly and stay healthy. Protein is the bodies 'building blocks' as it is found in every cell in the human body and is required to repair and maintain the body. Protein can come from many different sources including plant and animal products; to provide the body with all the nutrients it needs to function well, it is best to include a wide mixture of the different sources.

Types of protein:

Complete – These offer all 9 essential amino acids required to meet the needs of the human body.

Incomplete – These lack one or more of the essential amino acids and also tend to contain lower amounts of protein. This means these need to be combined with other protein sources to meet the needs of the body, and when combined, can form a complete protein. For example, combining rice and beans would form a complete protein source.

Some sources of protein include:

- Eggs
- Meat and poultry
- Dairy
- Soy Foods
- Buckwheat
- Quinoa
- Vegetables
- Cereals & Grains (wheat, rye, oats, rice)
- Nuts
- Pulses (lentils, beans & peas)

Carbohydrates

Carbohydrates provide the body with a fast source of energy; this is because they can be converted very quickly into glucose, a form of sugar, which the body uses as fuel. However, a diet too high in carbohydrates can have a negative effect on the bodies energy levels, causing spikes and dips in blood sugar levels leaving you feeling tired and grouchy after a crash!

The spike in the blood sugar levels is the same as that I referred to earlier when eating sugary foods, triggering the insulin release. In order to avoid the unsteady energy levels, it's best to try and stick to foods with a low glycaemic index (GI).

GI is how we refer to how quickly the energy from the food we eat is released into the blood stream and food is given a number 0 - 100 to show how quickly it is released, (100 being like eating pure sugar and giving you an instant hit).

Food that is highly processed, has had lots of cooking or is highly refined tends to have a higher GI, for example:

Lower GI	GI	Higher GI	GI
Brown Rice	45	Instant white rice	75
Sweet potato	50	Baked white potato	95
Rye bread	50	White bread	75
Maple syrup	55	White sugar	70

In my recipes I try to use lower GI alternatives where possible to keep the blood sugar levels nice and steady, this means you'll have slow release energy to keep you going and will be avoiding the mid-afternoon crash by replacing your high GI sandwich at lunch for something from my list of lovely lunches!

Hydration

Keeping hydrated is vitally important for all sorts of reasons as your body uses water for many of its functions; things like absorbing nutrients and even keeping joints in good condition. Over half of the body is made up of water which tells you just how important it is to keep your fluid levels topped up.
If you are trying to loose body fat, keeping well hydrated can also have a positive effect on the metabolism and drinking extra water before, during and after exercise also helps prevent dehydration and aids your body in its recovery.
The best way of keeping hydrated is by drinking...water! The cheapest, yet best drink; no calories or sugar, just pure hydration. Recommendations on how much you should drink vary on a daily basis, so aim to carry a bottle of water with you and sip away all day and also have a drink every time you eat, different people have different fluid needs but don't leave it until you're feeling thirsty!

I'm bored of drinking water...

Trying to keep well hydrated can sometimes seem like a chore so try mixing it up with these healthy flavourings for your water.

- Add frozen berries
- A lemon wedge
- Lime wedges and mint leaves
- Orange wedges

And if you're craving something fizzy, reach for the sparkling water instead of the fizzy pop, even the 'diet' versions are still full of baddies!

Tea & Coffee

Drinking lots of tea and coffee is something that many of us fall into without even realising it. Unfortunately, these favourites are packed with caffeine which gives the body a quick boost but then as that wears off a slump occurs. Drinking lots of caffeine causes the body to rely on these spikes to keep going, so to help you feel more energised and not waiting for your next caffeine hit, try replacing your tea and coffee with decaffeinated or even hot water with a slice of lemon.

Alcohol

Alcohol, unfortunately, has no positive effects on the body and has many negative, it:

- Dehydrates the body
- Increases appetite
- Reduces the body's ability to absorb nutrients, vitamins and minerals
- Increases the cortisol levels in the body, this is a stress hormone that also increases the storage of fat in the body
- Is often full of sugar and calories, for example, a large glass of wine can contain the same amount of calories as a slice of sponge cake!

It's sometimes hard to avoid alcohol completely, but do try to limit the amount you consume and if possible, cut it out altogether.

Meal Plans

The meal plans found at the end of the book give you an example of how you can combine the recipes from this book to create a day by day success plan.
I like to try and use up what I've made in the previous days, so as not to waste anything; so for each week you'll see some of the same things popping up a few times. If you make a batch of snacks at the start of the week or on a Sunday night, then they can fill any little gaps for the week.
Other snacks that are filling and tasty that don't involve much preparation include:

· **An apple with 1 tbsp peanut** butter *–this gives you one portion of fruit and also a little bit of protein to help kick the hunger*

· **A hardboiled egg** – *pop an egg on to boil whilst you sit and have your breakfast, packed full of protein*

· **Carrot or celery sticks with 1 tbsp hummus**- *again, getting in one of your 5 a day as well as being filling*

· **Handful of homemade granola & natural or Greek yoghurt** – *if you make a jar of granola and grab a handful as and when required, it's handy and very yummy!*

How do I fit in preparing meals?

Some good tips to make sure your busy lifestyle doesn't lead you off your path to success:

- Pick one evening a week that will be for making snacks that will last you for the week ahead.
- When you make meals like chilli, curry or lasagne, make double the size so you can freeze half and grab it from the freezer for a healthy 'ready meal'.
- Soups also freeze well, making a selection and keeping them in the freezer means you can reheat them for a warming convenient lunch.
- If you don't think you'll eat the whole loaf of bread you've made before it goes stale, cut it in half and freeze that too!

Running out of time on a morning and grabbing lunch on the go...

It's time to invest....in Tupperware, little plastic boxes will become your new best friend if you lead a busy life! Whilst your tea is cooking in the evening or before you go to bed, make your lunch and snacks for the next day, this will help you avoid getting 'food on the go' that is full of sugar and trans fats and will not provide your body with all the essential nutrients it needs to achieve your goals.

Symbols for success...

Throughout the book you will see symbols next to some of the recipes to help you out:

V — Vegetarian Meal – all the snacks are vegetarian too!

S — Speedy Supper- under 30mins to make and cook

P — 'Pack up and take with you' meals

F — Freezer safe

Reaching for the naughty snacks...

There will no doubt be hurdles you come across during your journey but keep in mind the end goal and how fantastic you will look and feel in your new body.
When you change your diet and exercise routine your body will be slightly surprised and you may feel a little tired for the first couple of days, but don't reach for the processed snacks to try and boost your energy, these will only give you a temporary boost but you will soon crash again. Try switching some snacks in your cupboards, for example...

· Biscuits **for** gluten free oat cakes
· Crisps **for** mixed nuts and seeds
· Chocolate bars **for** 80% + dark chocolate

Post Workout Fuel

Try and make sure you have one of your snacks containing protein or meals within an hour of completing a workout. This will help the muscles start to repair whilst also replenishing energy levels. If you are having a meal, rather than a snack, you should include some good carbs such as:

~ **Sweet potato** (150g = one portion have these as fries, mash or jacket)
~ **Brown rice** (1/2 cup dried = one portion)
~ **Quinoa** (1/2 cup dried = one portion)
~ **Wholegrain pasta** (1/2 cup dried = one portion)

But try to avoid eating these just before going to bed to allow the body to digest them, try and leave at least a couple of hours.

Impulse buys in the supermarket....

We all get to the supermarket and see the deals of the week and end up coming out with a trolley a lot fuller than we intended! To avoid your trolley being full of unhealthy foods, make a list before you go. I like to look through my meal plan for the week on a Sunday night and write down what ingredients I will need; this way you get what is necessary, don't get any naughty snacks and don't spend any more money than you have to! Here are my top ingredients to include in your shopping trolley:

Fresh		Cupboard	Meat, Fish & Dairy
Blueberries	Kale	Coconut oil	Free range eggs
Raspberries	Carrots	Quinoa	Free range chicken
Strawberries	Butternut squash	Oats	Salmon fillets
Bananas	Sweet potato	Coconut milk	Turkey mince / other lean mince
Kiwi Fruit	Hummus	Ground almonds	Lean beef stewing steak
Avocado	Lemons	Peanut butter	Cod / Haddock
Courgettes	Ginger	Oat cakes	Prawns
Celery	Basil	Cumin	Goats cheese
Mixed salad leaves	Garlic	Turmeric	Natural or Greek yoghurt
Cucumber	Spring onions	Paprika	
Tomatoes	Mushrooms	Honey	
Mixed Peppers	Chillies	Chinese 5 spice	
Onions		Soy sauce	
		Mixed nuts	
		Mixed seeds	

Breakfast

Chocolate Hazelnut Pancakes

Ingredients:

Serves 2

50g Hazelnuts
1 tbsp Oats
2 Eggs
1 Banana
1 tbsp Milled linseed (optional)
¼ tsp Baking powder
1 tsp Cocoa powder
1 tbsp Coconut oil

Method:

1. Blend hazelnuts and oats until they form a fine crumb.
2. Add all the other ingredients (apart from the coconut oil) and using a stick blender whizz into a batter.
3. Heat the coconut oil in a large frying pan on a medium heat.
4. Using a tablespoon place a spoon full at a time into the pan to make small pancakes.
5. Allow to cook until you see little bubbles on the surface, they are then ready to flip over.
6. Cook in batches and serve with juicy berries.
7. If you are just cooking for one, place half the pancakes in a freezer bag once they have cooled and freeze to use another day. I just pop them in the toaster when I'm ready to eat them!

Banana Pancakes

Ingredients:

Serves 1

2 Eggs
1 Banana
1 tbsp. Oats OR 3 tbsp. ground almonds
1 tbsp Coconut oil

To serve...

Blueberries/ raspberries / strawberries
Greek or natural yoghurt

Method:

1. Blend the banana, eggs and oats/ ground almonds together in a jug until smooth.
2. Melt the coconut oil in a frying pan on a medium heat and pour in the mixture in small circles (the size of little scotch pancakes!)
3. Allow pancakes to cook until you can run a spatula underneath to flip them over. Be careful not to burn them as they cook very quickly!
4. Serve with berries and natural or Greek yoghurt.

Poached Eggs & Avocado on Toast

Ingredients:

Serves 1

2 Eggs

½ a Ripe avocado

2 Small slices of wholegrain or rye bread

Salt and pepper

1 tsp Cider vinegar

Method:

1. Bring a pan of water to a gentle simmer then add the vinegar.
2. Crack one egg into a small dish or glass.
3. Stir the water until a 'whirlpool' forms in the middle.
4. Gently drop the egg into the centre of the whirlpool and allow to cook for a couple of minutes.
5. Whilst the egg is cooking, mash the avocado with a good grind of salt and pepper.
6. Lift the egg out, it should still be soft to press if you like your eggs runny.
7. Repeat with the other egg and toast the bread.

Salmon, 'Eggy' Avocado and Spinach

Ingredients:

Serves 1

1 Egg

30g of Smoked salmon

½ Avocado

Large handful spinach

1tsp Coconut oil

Salt and pepper

Method:

1. Warm the coconut oil in a pan, add the spinach with a grind of salt and pepper. Move the spinach around the pan until it has just wilted, this will only take a few minutes.
2. Remove and discard the stone from the avocado, slice a bit off the bottom of the avocado so it sits level on the baking tray.
3. Crack the egg into a ramekin then pour it into the centre of the avocado, (you may need to spoon out little of the avocado to make the hole bigger). Give a grind of salt and pepper.
4. Place under the grill at 200°C/180°C fan and cook until the egg is set and browned, this will only take a couple of minutes.
5. Serve together on a plate with the salmon, spinach and wedge of lemon.

Granola

Ingredients:

300g Nuts, (or use 150g oats & 100g nuts)
50g Pumpkin seeds and sunflower seeds mixed
2 tbsp Maple syrup or honey
1 Egg white
2 tbsp Coconut oil or olive oil
To serve...
Blueberries/ raspberries / strawberries
Greek or natural yoghurt

Method:

1. Preheat the oven to 150°C/130°C fan.
2. Place nuts in a blender a give a quick blast to break them up a little, be careful not to over blend otherwise they will become a powder. After they have been blended, place the nuts, (oats if using) and seeds in a large bowl and mix.
3. Heat the oil, syrup/honey slightly then pour over the nut mixture. Mix thoroughly, coating everything.
4. Whisk the egg white and pour over the oat mixture and again mix thoroughly.
5. Pour onto a lined baking tray and spread evenly, pressing the mixture down firmly.
6. Bake for 40mins or until golden all over. If you like smaller chunks, break up the granola after 20mins and return to the oven again.
7. Remove from oven then break up into desired size chunks and store in an air tight container.
8. Serve with berries and yoghurt or enjoy as a little snack between meals.

Porridge

Ingredients:

½ Mug oats
1 Mug of semi-skimmed milk or almond milk
½ Mug water
Optional toppings...
Cinnamon
Pumpkin seeds
Chia seeds
1 tsp Honey
Raspberries/ Strawberries/ Blueberries

Method:

1. Place the oats and milk in a saucepan on a gentle heat. If using the chia seeds add them now.
2. Keep stirring until the porridge thickens to the desired consistency.
3. Serve with a drizzle of honey and berries or any of the other toppings.

Feta Eggs

V

Ingredients

2 Eggs
1 Thumb sized piece of feta
1/2 Avocado
6 Cherry tomatoes
1/4 Red pepper
Large handful of spinach
Salt and pepper
Fresh basil (optional)
1 tsp Coconut oil

Method

1. Heat the coconut oil in a frying pan and chop the veg.
2. Once melted, add the veg and cook until soft.
3. Add the eggs with a good grind of salt and pepper then stir them quickly so they don't stick. Be careful not to overcook, remove from the heat whilst you stir if necessary.
4. Place the egg mixture on a plate then chop the avocado into cubes and scatter over the eggs.
5. Crumble the feta over and finally top with the fresh basil torn up into small strands.

Try and opt for free range eggs where possible, and even better if you can get hold of organic ones, the better the chicken eats and lives, the more goodness you get from their eggs!
This makes a great breakfast or lunch and is super filling, full of nutrients, protein and healthy fats!

Berry Omelette

Ingredients:

3 Eggs
2/3 cup Frozen or fresh berries
1 Ripe banana
1 tbsp Chia seeds (optional)
2 tsp Coconut oil
1 tsp Honey (optional)

Method:

1. Melt the oil in a frying pan on a medium heat. Blend the eggs with the banana then pour into the pan.
2. Sprinkle the berries and chia seeds over the top and allow the base of the omelette to cook.
3. Place under the grill for a couple of minutes to cook the top of the omelette.
4. Remove from pan when cooked then drizzle with honey, if using.

Bacon & Egg Fritters

Ingredients:

Serves 2
2 Eggs
2 tbsp Ground almonds
¼ Courgette
½ Red onion
Coconut oil
3 Mushrooms (or more if you like!)
1 Rasher of bacon chopped up
¼ tsp Baking powder
Salt & Pepper

Method:

1. Very finely chop all the veg.
2. Chop the bacon into small pieces and place in a frying pan with 1 tsp coconut oil and the chopped onion. Fry until both are cooked.
3. Place chopped veg, cooked bacon, onion, baking powder, ground almonds and a good grind of salt and pepper in a large bowl and stir well.
4. Add the eggs and stir well again.
5. Heat 1 tbsp of coconut oil in a frying pan then place a large spoonful of mixture into the pan to form a fritter. Repeat until you have formed 6 fritters. You may have to cook in batches.
6. Cook for a couple of minutes on one side then flip over and cook on the other side. Both sides should be nicely coloured.

Pesto Pancakes

Ingredients:

¼ cup Brazil nuts
A large handful of basil leaves
1 Clove of garlic
1 tsp Olive oil
A squeeze of lemon juice
Flesh of half an avocado
3 tbsp Ground almonds
2 Eggs
½ tsp Baking powder
A grind of salt
1 tbsp Coconut oil

Method:

1. Place the nuts, chopped garlic clove, basil, olive oil and lemon juice in a blender and blend to a smooth paste.
2. Add all the remaining ingredients apart from the coconut oil and blend again.
3. Heat the coconut oil in a large frying pan on a medium heat.
4. Spoon the mixture into the pan in small pancakes and allow to cook for a couple of minutes before flipping over and cooking on the other side.
5. Serve with grilled cherry tomatoes.

Dippy Eggs and Asparagus

Ingredients:

2 Eggs
4 Asparagus spears

Method:

1. Bring a pan of water to a gentle boil. Place one egg at a time on a slotted spoon and dip them in the water then take out for a few seconds. Repeat a couple of times before leaving the egg in the water. This method should help prevent the eggs from cracking.
2. Cook the eggs for 4 minutes (they should still be runny), you can also steam the asparagus over the eggs for about the same time. If you like them more well done or they are quite chunky pop them on a couple of minutes before the eggs. Alternatively, place the asparagus spears, cut in half, in a griddle pan on a medium heat until they are coloured after a couple of minutes steaming.
3. Remove the eggs from the water and place in egg cups, remove the top of the egg to make a hole to dip your asparagus spears in.

Sweet Potato Hash Brown with a Poached Egg & Salmon

Ingredients

1 Egg
1/3 Medium sweet potato
1 Spring onion
6 Cherry tomatoes
1 slice Smoked salmon
Large handful of spinach
Pepper
2 tsp Coconut oil
Glug of white wine vinegar

Method

1. Peel the sweet potato and cut into cubes, you can pop these into the microwave for a few minutes to soften or in a pan of boiling water on the hob.
2. Once the potato is soft enough to mash up with a fork it is ready.
3. Heat 1 tsp coconut oil in a frying pan then add the spring onion and cook until it becomes soft.
4. Add the onion to the potato and combine the two. Using your hands (make sure the mixture is cool enough to handle!) form a little pattie about 1.5cm thick.
5. Heat the remaining coconut oil in the frying pan and pop the hash brown in so it can colour, flip over and let the other side colour too. Whilst this is cooking, pop your egg in to poach.
6. Bring a pan of water to a gentle simmer then add a glug of the vinegar.
7. Crack one egg into a small dish or glass.
8. Stir the water until a 'whirlpool' forms in the middle.
9. Gently drop the egg into the centre of the whirlpool and allow to cook for a couple of minutes.
10. Lift the egg out, it should still be soft to press if you like your eggs runny.
11. Remove the hash brown from the pan and throw in the spinach and tomatoes and cook until the spinach softens.
12. Start stacking you breakfast in any order you like, adding the salmon in along the way!

Lunch

Pastry Free Quiche

Ingredients:

6 Eggs
1 Small courgette
1 Red pepper
1 Yellow pepper
1 Red onion
Cheese - 40g goats cheese /cheddar/ other
2 tbsp Pine nuts (Optional)
Salt and pepper
1 tbsp Coconut oil

Method:

1. Heat oven to 170°C/150°C fan. Chop the veg and place in a frying pan with the coconut oil on a medium heat.
2. Whilst veg is cooking, line a loaf tin with greaseproof paper and break the eggs into a jug and whisk. Add salt and pepper.
3. Once veg is cooked sprinkle half of it into the base of the loaf tin, pour the egg mixture in and add the remaining veg.
4. Sprinkle or add the cheese, depending on which sort you are using. Place in the oven for 30 mins.
5. When the quiche stays still when you move the tin, add the pine nuts and cook for a few more minutes until the pine nuts are golden.

Curried Quinoa

Ingredients

1/4 cup of quinoa
1 Turkey / chicken breast chopped up (optional)
Mixed veg (1/4 courgette, 6 cherry tomatoes,1/4 red pepper, 2 spring onions)
1 Large handful of spinach
1 tsp Curry powder (p112) or 1 tsp turmeric
1 tsp Coconut oil

Method

1. Place the quinoa in a pan of simmering water and leave to cook for about 15-20mins or until the quinoa is soft and fully puffed up. Once cooked, remove from the heat and drain.
2. Chop the veg up into small cubes, leaving the spinach leaves whole.
3. In a frying pan, melt the coconut oil then add the turkey or chicken to the pan. Once the meat is cooked add the veg, leaving the spinach until later.
4. Once the veg starts to soften, add the curry powder (or turmeric) and stir well to coat all the veg. Add the cooked quinoa and spinach to the frying pan and stir well until the leaves of spinach soften and the quinoa is coated with spice.
6. This is a great meal to make a double portion and keep in the fridge for the next day, can be eaten hot or cold.

Goats Cheese and Peas on Toast

Ingredients:

Serves one

50g Goats cheese

3 tbsp Frozen garden peas

2 tbsp Pine nuts

4 Cherry tomatoes

Handful basil leaves

2 Slices homemade rye bread

Method:

1. Place the peas in a sieve and defrost by pouring hot water over them. Leave to drain.
2. Cut in half the tomatoes and place on a tray under the grill until they start to soften. Remove from the grill.
3. Cut two slices of bread and toast. Meanwhile mix the peas and goats cheese, then spread on the toast once cooked.
4. Place the tomatoes with the pine nuts on top of the cheese on the toast then return to the grill to finish the tomatoes off and brown the nuts...they don't take long so watch them carefully!
5. Serve with basil leaves sprinkled on top!

Salad combinations for quick lunches

Mixed Beans and Goats Cheese - 200g mixed beans & 1tbsp goats cheese

Salmon & Pomegranate seeds - 1 cooked salmon fillet with 2 tbsp pomegranate seeds

Ham & Cottage Cheese- 2 slices of home cooked ham & 1 tbsp cottage cheese

Grilled Chicken & Hummus - 1 grilled chicken breast, 1 tbsp hummus

Pesto Chicken - 1 grilled chicken breast, 1 tbsp pesto (p114) & 1/2 avocado cubed

Pesto Prawns - 1 cup cooked prawns, 1 tbsp pesto (p114)

Moroccan chicken / salmon - rub the chicken or fish with 1 tsp of spice mix before cooking. (p110)

Fig and Mozzarella- 1 fig, 50g mozzarella, 2 tbsp macadamia nuts, 1 tbsp balsamic vinegar. Place the sliced fig and macadamia nuts under the grill to lightly toast then serve with the mozzarella and balsamic vinegar on a bed of leaves.

Serve any of these combinations with mixed lettuce leaves, avocado, tomatoes, sweetcorn, cucumber, celery, avocado, toasted seeds and nuts such as pumpkin or pine nuts. Or place one of these tasty fillings in a wrap or rye bread sandwich.

Warm Kale and Halloumi Salad

Ingredients:

Serves 1

4/5 Slices of halloumi, 1cm thick
2 Tomatoes
2 Spring onions
1 tbsp Pumpkin seeds
1 tbsp Macadamia nuts
3 Sun dried tomatoes
Salt and pepper
1 tbsp Coconut oil

Method

1. Place the coconut oil in a large frying pan on a medium heat. Once it has melted, chop the sundried tomatoes and add them to the pan.
2. Cook the sun dried tomatoes for a couple of minutes then add the spring onion and tomatoes.
3. Cook for a couple more minutes, then add the macadamia nuts and cook until the tomatoes become very soft and you can mash them up.
4. Add the kale and allow to steam slightly.
5. After a minute or two of steaming, mix the kale in and cook until the kale is soft.
6. Add the pumpkin seeds and cook for two more minutes, then remove from the heat and place in a bowl.
7. Place the sliced halloumi in the same pan and brown on each side slightly, then remove from the pan and place on top of the kale salad.

Thai Red Prawns and Veg

Ingredients:

Serves one

1 tbsp. Coconut oil
1 tbsp. Thai red curry paste (p107)
1/2 Red pepper
½ Courgette
½ Red onion
Handful of mushrooms
100g Sweetcorn
150g King prawns
1 tbsp. Crème fraiche

Method:

1. Place coconut oil in a pan, once melted add the veg and cook for a couple of minutes.
2. Add the red curry paste and cook until veg is just about ready.
3. Finally, add the prawns and the crème fraiche and stir until prawns are cooked through and piping hot. Serve and enjoy!

Goats Cheese and Roast Peppers

Ingredients:

Serves one

2 Goats cheese discs

6 or more Cherry tomatoes

1 Bell Pepper (any colour)

Mixed Salad Leaves

Cucumber

Celery

Pine Nuts

Method:

1. Turn the grill up to 200°C/180°C fan.
2. Line a tray with greaseproof paper, chop the pepper into strips and place them on the tray with the tomatoes and place under the grill.
3. When they start to brown, remove from the oven and place the two discs of goats cheese on the tray with the veg and place them back under the grill.
4. While the cheese is browning, place the salad leaves, chopped cucumber and chopped celery in a large bowl.
5. Once the cheese starts to bubble and colour, remove from the heat.
6. Place the cheese, peppers and tomatoes on the bed of salad. Sprinkle the pine nuts on the tray and pop under the grill for 1 minute or until lightly browned...they don't take long so watch them carefully! Sprinkle them on the salad and enjoy!

Cooked Halloumi, Peppers and Pine nuts

Ingredients:

Serves one

100g Halloumi, sliced into 1cm thick discs

½ Red pepper

3 Sundried tomatoes

2 tbsp Pine nuts

Rocket / lettuce

Cherry tomatoes

1 tbsp Coconut oil

Method:

1. Place the coconut oil in a frying pan, once melted add the pepper and the halloumi. Place the rocket and cherry tomatoes in a large bowl.
2. Allow halloumi to cook for a couple of minutes or until the cheese has browned then flip over. Once browned on each side, place on the bed of salad.
4. Do the same with the red pepper, let it colour then place on the salad.
5. In the same pan, place the sundried tomatoes and pine nuts, cook until the nuts have coloured then sprinkle over the salad and enjoy!

Pesto Frittata

V

Ingredients

3 Eggs (whisked)
1/2 Red onion
1/2 Cup mushrooms
4 Stems of broccoli
2 Handfuls of spinach
1 tbsp Pesto (p114)
30g Goats cheese or 2 tbsp cottage cheese
1 tsp Coconut oil

Method

1. Steam the broccoli for a few of minutes or until it is soft enough for your liking.
2. Melt the coconut oil in a frying pan on a medium heat then add the chopped onion and mushrooms.
3. Cook until they become soft then add the spinach and allow to cook down.
4. Add the egg, stir once then place the broccoli on top and allow to cook for a couple of minutes.
5. Place under the grill until the top colours, serve with some goats cheese dotted on top.

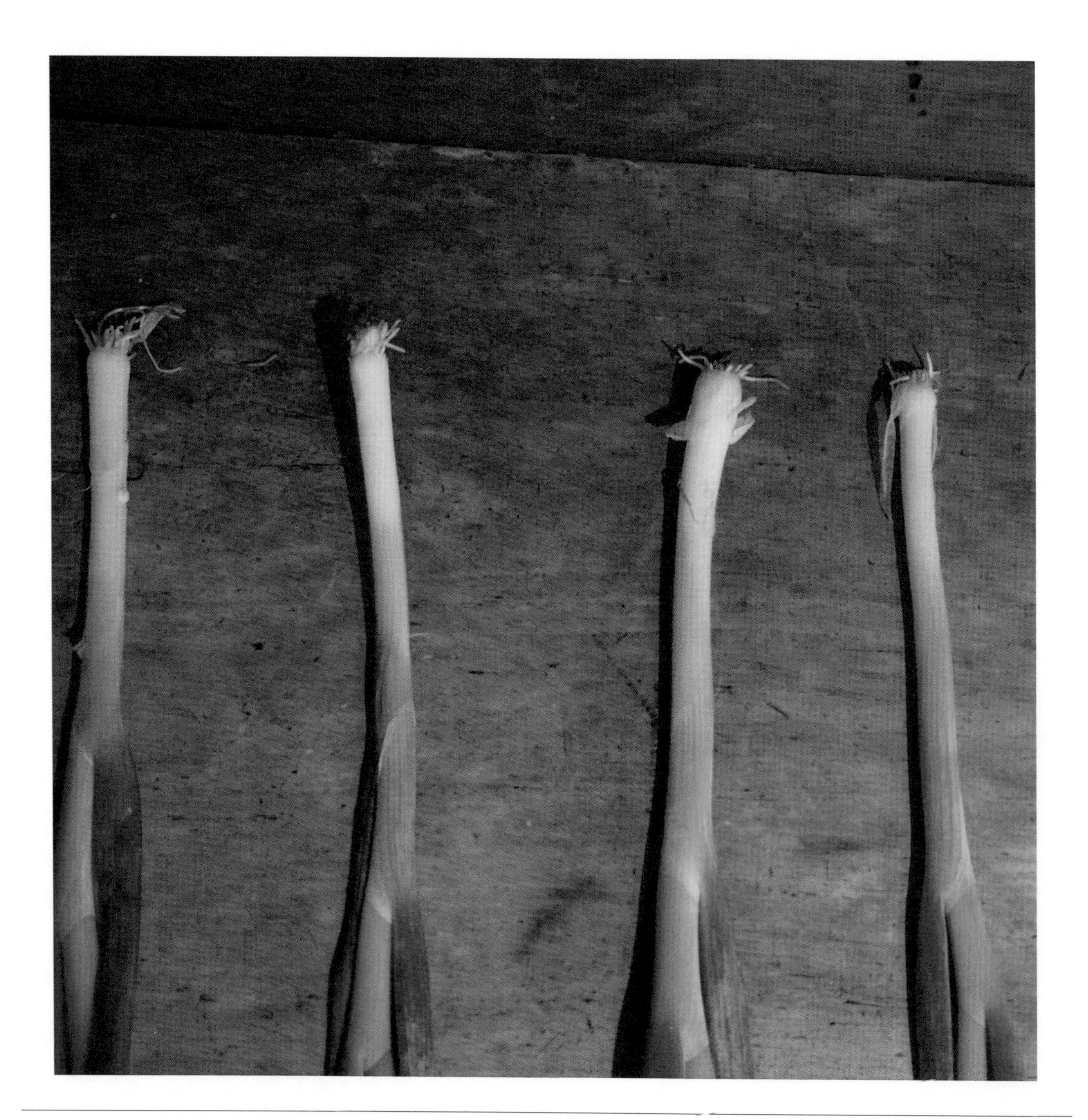

Soup and Bread

Thai Pumpkin Soup

F

V

Ingredients:

1 Large clove of garlic
1 Large red onion diced
1 Thumb sized piece of ginger
2 Small chillies finely chopped
1kg Pumpkin or squash, peeled
2 Carrots, peeled
1 Sweet potato, peeled
2 tsp Turmeric
Juice of one lemon
Handful of fresh coriander
2 tbsp Fish sauce
6 large Fresh basil leaves
1L Chicken or veg stock
1 tbsp Coconut oil

Method:

1. Heat the oil in a large pan then add the chopped garlic, ginger, onion and chillies and fry for a few minutes.
2. Cube the pumpkin, carrot and sweet potato and add these to the pan. Stir well then add the turmeric, lemon juice, chopped coriander, basil and the fish sauce.
3. Stir for a minute before adding the chicken stock and a good grind of salt and pepper.
4. Allow to simmer for 40 mins or until pumpkin is soft, then blend and serve! I like to serve with toasted pumpkin seeds (bought) sprinkled on the top.

Carrot & Coriander Soup

Ingredients:
1 Red onion
1 tsp Ground coriander
4 Carrots
1 Clove of garlic
1 Litre veg stock
3 tbsp Chopped fresh coriander
Salt and pepper
1 tbsp Coconut oil

Method:
1. Heat the oil in a large pan, add chopped onions, garlic and carrots and sauté until they begin to soften.
2. Stir in the ground coriander and salt and pepper and cook for 1 min.
3. Add stock and bring to the boil, simmer for about 20mins or until all the veg is soft, then stir in the fresh coriander.
4. Blend and season to taste.

Spicy Sweet Potato and Butternut Soup

Ingredients:
1 Butternut squash
2 Carrots
1 Red onion
1 Large sweet potato
Sprig of rosemary
½ tsp Turmeric
½ tsp Chilli powder
½ tsp Paprika
Handful of fresh coriander chopped
2 Bay leaves
500ml Chicken or veg stock
Salt and pepper
1 tbsp Coconut oil

Method:
1. Fry the herbs and spices in the coconut oil with the chopped onion over a medium heat.
2. Add the chopped carrots, cubed squash and sweet potato and stir until fully coated in herbs and spices.
3. Add the chicken stock, salt and pepper and simmer for 45 minutes then blend until smooth.

Tomato & Basil Soup

Ingredients:
1kg Tomatoes
1 Clove of garlic
Pinch of sea salt
1 Carrot
1 Celery stick
1 Red onion
500ml Chicken or veg stock
Handful of fresh basil chopped
1 tbsp Coconut oil
Black pepper

Method:
1. Cut the tomatoes in half and place on a baking tray
2. Crush the garlic and sea salt together and sprinkle on the tomatoes.
3. Bake in the oven at 200°C/180°C fan for 40mins.
4. Chop the carrots, celery and onion into small cubes. Heat oil in the pan and add chopped veg.
5. Cook until softened then add the stock and basil, simmer for 10mins then remove from heat.
6. Remove the tomatoes from the oven and add to the veg and stock, blend until smooth.

Courgette & Spinach Soup

Ingredients:
1 Celery stick
2 Garlic cloves
2 Red onions
500g Courgette (2 medium courgettes) chopped
200g Potatoes, peeled and chopped
1 Large handful of basil
150g Spinach
500ml Veg stock
Salt and pepper
1 tbsp Coconut oil

Method:
1. Chop the onion, garlic and celery and sauté in the coconut oil.
2. Once the onion softens, add the courgette and potatoes and cook for a couple of minutes. Add the stock, a good grind of pepper, chopped basil and spinach then simmer for 30mins.
3. Take off the heat and blend, add a dash of cream to serve!

Super Greens Soup

Ingredients:

1 Red onion
1 Clove of garlic
1 Head of broccoli
220g Green beans
1 Cup of garden peas
1 Medium white potato, peeled and cubed
1 Litre veg stock
Large handful of chopped basil (optional)
Salt and pepper
1 tbsp coconut oil

Method:

1. Heat the coconut oil in a large pan, add the chopped onion and garlic and sauté until they begin to soften.
2. Chop the broccoli into small florets and the beans in half then add to the pan, along with the potato.
3. Add stock and bring to the boil, then add the peas, salt, pepper and basil.
4. Simmer until all veg is soft (about 25 mins) then blend and season to taste.

Tip: If you want to make your soup more of a filling meal, try boiling an egg for 6mins and serving on top of the soup.

Mediterranean Bread

Ingredients:
350g Wholemeal flour
50g Rye flour
1 Packet of yeast (7g)
1 tsp Salt
3 tsp Tomato purée
30g Sundried tomatoes
5 tbsp. Olive oil
140ml Warm water
Handful Fresh basil Chopped finely
2 tsp Dried or fresh rosemary

Method:
1. Mix flour, salt and yeast in a bowl then make a well in the middle.
2. Add half the water to the well and mix well. Add the purée and remaining water then mix well again.
3. Add oil and herbs then knead the dough for 5mins.
4. Place back in the bowl, cover with cling film then leave to rise for an hour or until doubled in size in a warm place.
5. Knead in the sun dried tomatoes and make into small rolls or form a large plait.
6. Bake at 200°C/180°C fan until sounds hollow when tapped on the bottom.

Rye Bread

Ingredients:
400g Rye flour
200g Wholemeal flour
1 tsp Yeast
1 tbsp Molasses
1 tsp Salt
2 tbsp Oil
450ml Warm water

Method:
1.Place the molasses in the warm water and still until well mixed
2. In a bowl, mix the two flours, yeast and salt. Pour in the water mixture and oil and mix to a dough.
5. Knead for a couple of minutes then place back in bowl and cover with cling film and leave in a warm place for 45mins - an hour.
6. Take out of bowl and knead again for 5 minutes then form a circular loaf and place on a baking tray.
7. Using a sharp knife, mark a cross in the top of the loaf and leave to rise again for 30mins - 45mins before placing in the oven for 45 minutes at 220°C/200°C fan. The loaf should sound hollow when you tap the bottom.

Main Meals

PESTO
GOATS
CHEESE
FREE RANGE
CHICKEN
COURGETTE

Pesto Chicken & Courgetti

S

Ingredients

Serves 2

2 Chicken breasts
2 Medium courgettes
2 tbsp Pesto (p114)
50g Goats cheese
1 tbsp Coconut oil

Method

1. Make the courgetti using a spiralizer or by cutting the courgette up into very fine strands.
2. Melt the coconut oil in a frying pan on a medium heat. Cut the chicken breasts in half and add to the pan, colour on all sides.
3. Wrap the chicken in foil and place in the oven at 180°C/160°C fan for 20 mins or until the chicken is cooked through.
4. Place the courgetti in a pan of boiling water for 2 minutes so that it becomes soft and spaghetti like.
5. Drain the courgetti and add the pesto, stir well and serve with the chicken. Garnish with crumbled goats cheese!

Fish Curry

Ingredients:

Serves 2

2 Large white fish fillets, frozen or fresh (cod, basa or haddock)
1 Green pepper
Handful baby corn
6 Mushrooms
1 Large white onion
1 Clove of garlic
1 Chilli (optional)
1 Can coconut milk
1 tbsp Curry powder (p112) (or 2tsp ground turmeric & 1tsp cumin)
1 tbsp Coconut oil
Salt & pepper

Method:

1. Heat the coconut oil in a large pan on a medium heat, then add the curry powder and stir.
2. Chop the veg and add to the pan, along with the garlic (crushed) and the chilli (finely chopped).
3. Keep stirring until the onion starts to soften then add the coconut milk and a good grind of salt and pepper.
4. Bring to a simmer then add the fish, place a lid on the pan and leave to simmer for 20 mins if fresh, 25mins if frozen.
5. Serve with quinoa or rice.

F

Meatballs

Ingredients:

Serves 4

Meatballs

500g Low fat mince (turkey or beef)

1 tsp Oregano

1 Clove of garlic, crushed

Salt and pepper

2 Eggs

1 tbsp Coconut oil

Sauce

1 Carton passata

1 Clove of garlic

Handful of fresh basil

1/2 cup Mushrooms

1 Yellow pepper

1 White onion, finely chopped

1 tsp Coconut oil

Method

1. Combine all meatball ingredients (apart from coconut oil) in a bowl and form 4cm diameter meatballs. TIP- if you wet your hands it makes forming the balls easier!
2. In a pan on a medium heat, heat the oil, add the meatballs and cook all over, for approximately 5 minutes.
3. Once meatballs are cooked, remove from pan and add 1 tsp of coconut oil, the garlic, basil, mushrooms, pepper and onion and cook until veg is soft.
4. Add the passata, stock cube, a grind of pepper, and the meatballs and leave to simmer for 10 minutes. Serve with salad, courgetti or wholegrain spaghetti.

Homemade Chicken Kiev

Ingredients:

Serves 2

2 Large chicken breasts

2 tbsp Pesto (p114)

Wholemeal flour

1 Egg

Veg to serve

Method:

1. Make a deep slice along the side of the chicken breast and stuff 1 tbsp of pesto, repeat for the second chicken breast.
2. Close the chicken up then roll it in whisked egg and then wholemeal flour. Place in the oven for 35mins at 190°C/170°C fan.
3. After 20mins take it out the oven and spoon some of the tasty juices over the chicken then return to the oven for the final 15mins! Serve with veg.

S

Pesto Veg & Basa

Ingredients:

Serves 2

2 Basa / sea bass or any white fish fillets

250g King prawns

1 Yellow pepper

½ Courgette

1 Leek

Asparagus

2 tbsp Pesto (p114)

1 tbsp Coconut oil

Method:

1. Dice the veg and parboil the asparagus, then sauté all together with the coconut oil in a large frying pan
2. Once cooked remove from pan and set aside. Now use the same pan to cook the fish over a medium heat for about 5mins on each side. Add a splash of olive oil or a little more coconut oil if pan is very dry. Once the fish is cooked, remove from pan and wrap in foil.
3. Add veg back to pan along with the king prawns. Add the pesto, stir well and cook for 5 minutes or until prawns are cooked. Remove the pan from the heat and serve the veg and prawns with the fish.

F

S

Turkey Mince Bolognaise

Ingredients:

Serves 3 / 4

500g Turkey mince

1 Large white onion, finely chopped

1/2 cup Mushrooms

1 Yellow or red pepper

1 Carrot

1 Clove of garlic

Handful of basil

1 tsp Oregano

One beef stock cube

Salt & Pepper

1 Carton of passata or 1 can of chopped tinned tomatoes

Method:

1. Place a large pan on a medium heat and add the mince. Cook until coloured.
2. Add the onion, carrot, garlic and herbs and cook for a few minutes.
3. Add the rest of the veg, stock cube, salt and pepper and the passata.
4. Allow to simmer for at least 15 minutes, the longer the better to allow the flavours to come out!
5. Serve with salad, wholegrain spaghetti or courgetti.

Salmon with Thai Green Veg

Ingredients:

Serves 2

2 Salmon fillets

½ Large courgette

1 Red pepper

Broccoli

Cup of baby corn

Cup of sugar snap peas

Handful of Cashew Nuts (optional)

2 tbsp Thai green curry paste (p87)

1 tbsp Coconut oil

Method:

1. Heat the oven to 200°C/180°C fan.
2. Place the salmon skin side down on a tray lined with foil. Rub 1tbsp Thai green curry paste over the salmon, then wrap in foil and place in the oven for 15 minutes to cook.
3. Meanwhile, pop the broccoli and baby corn on to steam for 5-7 minutes depending on how you like your veg cooked.
4. Finely slice the pepper and place in a pan with the coconut oil on a medium heat.
5. Add the cashew nuts, if using. As the veg starts to soften, add a tablespoon of Thai paste and continue to cook until veg is done.
6. Throw in the baby corn and broccoli, stir well then serve with the salmon.

Chickpea and Spinach Casserole

Ingredients:

Serves 2

2 Chicken breasts (Optional)

250g Spinach or kale

1 x 400g Can of chickpeas

1 Thumb sized piece of chorizo sausage, cut into small chunks (optional)

I 500g Carton passata or 1 400g tin chopped tomatoes

1 Garlic clove (chopped and crushed)

1 Onion (finely chopped)

1 Carrot (chopped)

1 Chicken or vegetable stock cube

1 tsp Smoked paprika

Thyme, salt and pepper

1 tbsp Coconut oil

Method:

1. Add the coconut oil to a large pan, throw in the chicken (diced), onion, carrot, garlic and chorizo and fry for about 10 minutes or until chicken is cooked.
2. Add passata, stock cube and seasonings, bring to the boil and add chickpeas and spinach.
3. Turn down heat and bring to a gentle simmer and cook for a further 15 mins or leave in the oven at 180°C/160°C fan for 15mins.

Serve with veg such as broccoli, green beans or asparagus.

Frittata

V

S

Ingredients:

Serves 1

4 Eggs

Smoked salmon slices or 1 fillet (optional)

5 Asparagus spears

Pepper, mushrooms, tomatoes or any veg you fancy

25g Grated cheese

1 Red onion

Salt and pepper

1 tsp Coconut oil

Method:

1. Place asparagus spears over a steamer or in a pan of boiling water and cook until ready to eat, (5-7mins)
2. Using the coconut oil, fry the onion and veg in an oven proof frying pan.
3. Once cooked, add the salmon for a couple of minutes or until heated right through if using.
4. Whisk the eggs with the herbs, seasoning and cheese and pour over fried veg and salmon, arrange the asparagus on the top and cook for a few minutes or until egg starts to look cooked. To finish off, place under the grill to cook the top half of the frittata.

Smoked Haddock & Stir Fry Veg with Lemon Quinoa

S

Ingredients:

Serves 2

2 Smoked haddock fillets
1 Yellow pepper
1 Broccoli head
½ Pack of sugar snap peas
100g Baby corn
1 Red onion
1 Lemon
1 Thumb sized piece of ginger
1 Clove of garlic, crushed
1 tsp Soy sauce
2 tsp Chinese five spice
1 tsp Honey
½ Cup of quinoa
Salt and pepper
1 tbsp Coconut oil

Method

1. Turn the oven up to 180°C/160°C fan. Place the haddock skin side down on foil and wrap up, place in the oven for 20mins.
2. Place the quinoa in a pan with a squeeze of lemon juice and a grind of salt and cover with boiling water. Leave to simmer for about 15 -20mins until cooked.
3. Chop the veg into strips and the broccoli into florets. Place the florets in a pan of boiling water or over a steamer until they are almost cooked.
4. Place the coconut oil in a wok then add the ginger (minced), garlic and onion and fry for one minute.
5. Add all the veg along with a squeeze of lemon juice, the soy sauce, the honey, five spice and some salt and pepper.
6. Once the veg is cooked, serve with the fish and drained quinoa.

Lentil and Bean Casserole

Ingredients

Serves 2

150g Green lentils
400g Tin of mixed beans
1 Large onion
1 Clove of garlic
6 Sundried tomatoes
1 x 500g Carton of passata
1/2 cup Mushrooms
1/2 Courgette
Handful of fresh basil
100g Spinach
Juice of half a lemon
Salt and pepper
1 tbsp Coconut oil

Method

1. Preheat the oven to 180°C/160°C fan. Rinse the lentils then place them in a pan and cover with water. Simmer for 10 minutes then drain.
2. Heat the coconut oil in an oven proof pan, then add the chopped onion, chopped garlic and sun dried tomatoes and keep stirring.
3. Add the mushrooms and courgette, then the mixed beans.
4. Stir well then add the lentils, chopped basil and passata.
5. Give a good grind of salt and pepper then finally add the spinach, stir well and place in the oven for 30 mins.
6. Remove from the oven, squeeze in the juice of half a lemon and stir well. Serve with greens.

SALMON
BROCCOLI
MINT
ASPARAGUS

Cajun Spiced Salmon

Ingredients

Serves 2

2 Salmon fillets
1/2 Head of broccoli
8 Asparagus spears
1 tbsp Cajun spice (p114)
1 tbsp Coconut oil
3 tbsp Natural yoghurt
Handful of fresh mint

Method

1. Melt the coconut oil in a frying pan on a medium heat. Rub the spice mix over the salmon and place it in the pan skin side down.
2. Allow the salmon to cook for a few minutes on each side then pop in the oven at 180°C/160°C fan for 10 minutes. Keep the pan out for the veg.
3. Steam the broccoli and asparagus until they are as soft or crunchy as you like them, then pop them in the same pan you cooked the salmon in for a couple of minutes, turning them as they colour on a medium heat.
4. Finely chop the mint and mix it in with the yoghurt.
5. Combine together on a plate and enjoy!

V

Buckwheat Risotto

Ingredients

Serves 2/3
170g Buckwheat
1/2 Small butternut squash
1 Red onion, chopped
1 Garlic clove, very finely chopped
250ml Chicken stock
1 cup Garden peas
½ Head of broccoli
Juice of half lemon
250g King prawns (optional)
Salt and pepper
Parmesan (optional)

Method:

1. Sauté the onions in the coconut oil, after a couple of minutes, add the garlic, a pinch of salt, pepper, the cubed squash and the buckwheat.
2. Allow to cook for a couple of minutes then pour in the stock and simmer for 10 minutes.
3. Add the broccoli and peas and simmer for another ten minutes, stirring regularly.
4. After 5 minutes, add the prawns and lemon juice and continue to stir regularly.
5. After the final 5 minutes, check the buckwheat is soft before removing from the heat. Grate a small amount of parmesan on top to garnish.

Lamb Stew

Ingredients

Serves 2

2 Large lamb chops
3 Carrots
1 Large onion
2 Garlic cloves
1/2 Large courgette
150g Green beans
1 Sprig of fresh rosemary or 1 tsp dried rosemary
1 Sprig of fresh thyme or 1 tsp dried thyme
Salt and pepper
1 tbsp Coconut oil
1 tbsp Wholegrain mustard

Method:

1. Sauté the onions in the coconut oil, after a couple of minutes, add the garlic and lamb chops and stir until they begin to colour.
2. Add the chopped carrots and courgette. Remove the leaves of the herbs from the stem, finely chop and add them to the pan. Pour in the hot water, add the mustard and stir well.
3. Bring to a simmer then either place in the oven at 180°C/160°C fan for 40mins or leave to simmer gently on the hob.
4. After 40mins, add the green beans and return to the heat for 10 minutes before serving.

Lamb Chops

Ingredients:

Serves 2

2 Large lamb chops
3 Fresh rosemary sprigs
1 tsp Dried thyme
2 Garlic cloves
1 tsp English mustard
1 tbsp Water
2 tbsp. Lightly crushed macadamia nuts (optional)
1 tbsp Coconut oil

Method:

1. Crush the garlic, chop the rosemary and mix together with the mustard, water and thyme.
2. Rub the mixture over the lamb chops and leave to marinade for at least an hour.
3. Heat the coconut oil in a large frying pan on a medium heat.
4. When melted place the chops in the pan and cook for about 7 minutes, then turn over and cook for a further 5 minutes.
5. When there is just a couple of minutes left, add the macadamia nuts and brown them. Serve the lamb with some fresh veg.

Rosemary & Lemon Chicken

Ingredients:

Serves 2

2 Large chicken breasts
3 Large sprigs of rosemary (1 sprig finely chopped)
1 Red onion, chopped
1 Lemon, halved
Salt and pepper
1 tbsp Coconut oil

Method:

1. Heat the oven to 200°C/180°C fan. Place the coconut oil in frying pan on a medium heat.
2. Once it has melted add the chicken breasts and start to cook, keep moving them in the pan so they don't stick.
3. Throw in the chopped rosemary and onions and cook with the chicken until it has coloured on all sides. Place the chicken in an oven proof dish with the cooked herbs and onion.
4. Squeeze the juice of the lemon over the chicken then place the two halves of the lemon in the dish with the chicken. Place the 2 left over sprigs of rosemary in the dish as well then give the chicken a good grind of salt and pepper.
5. Cover the dish with foil and place in the oven for 35-40mins. Check the chicken is cooked all the way through before serving with some crunchy salad!

Stir Fry

Ingredients:

Serves 2/3

2 Chicken breasts or 400g diced pork or 400g diced beef or 250g prawns (Optional)
50g Cashew nuts
1 Red onion
A selection of veg - mushrooms, carrots, sugar snap peas, courgette, peppers
1 Clove of garlic
2 tsp Chinese five spice
1 tbsp Soy sauce
1 tsp Honey
1 tsp Grated ginger
1 tbsp Sesame seeds
Salt and pepper
1 tbsp Coconut oil

Method:

1. Place the coconut oil in a wok or large frying pan, once heated, add the meat unless using prawns, these are best added towards the end.
2. Allow the meat to cook through then add garlic and ginger and cook for a few minutes. Add the veg and allow to start softening. At this point add the prawns if using.
3. Add the remaining ingredients, stir well. Once veg is fully cooked, remove from heat and serve.

Lasagne

Ingredients:

Serves 4

500g Lean mince (beef or turkey)
1 Red Onion, finely chopped
1 400g Tin of chopped tomatoes or 1 carton of passata
250g Spinach
150g Ricotta or goats cheese
1 Red pepper, very finely chopped
1/2 cup Mushrooms
1 tsp Oregano
Handful fresh basil
1 Clove of garlic
2 tbsp pine nuts (optional)
Beef stock cube
Salt & Pepper

Method

1. Preheat the oven to 200°C/180°C fan. Dry fry the mince in a large pan, with the onion, pepper, mushrooms and crushed garlic and cook until veg is soft.
2. Add the chopped tomatoes (or passata), herbs, salt and pepper and stock cube. Allow to simmer for at least 10 minutes.
3. Place 1/3 of the mince in the bottom of a dish then layer a third of the spinach on top. Repeat twice more and spread the ricotta on the top layer of spinach.
4. Place dish in the oven and bake until the cheese starts to colour. For the final couple of minutes, sprinkle the pine nuts over the top and brown them. Watch them carefully as they cook very quickly! Remove from the oven and serve with salad.

Chilli

F

S

Ingredients:

Serves 4

500g Lean mince (Turkey or beef)
1 White Onion, finely chopped
1 400g Tinned tomatoes
½ tsp Ground cumin
1 tsp Smoked paprika
1-2 tsp Chilli powder
1 400g Can kidney beans
70g or 1/3 cup of wholegrain rice per person
1 tbsp Coconut oil
1 Beef stock cube

Method

1. Dry fry the mince in a large pan, once the mince is almost cooked, add the onion, the cumin, the paprika and the chilli powder.
2. Stirring regularly, allow to cook until the onion softens then add the beef stock cube.
3. Add the kidney beans, tinned tomatoes and ½ cup of boiling water and allow to simmer for at least 15 minutes. Whilst the chilli is cooking, put the rice on to boil then serve together. The longer the chilli has to cook the better it will taste!

Chicken Korma

F

Ingredients

Serves 2

2 Chicken breasts, chopped into large cubes
1 Large white onion
1 Thumb sized piece of ginger, peeled and grated
1 Garlic clove, peeled and finely chopped
1 Yellow pepper, diced
1/2 Cup of chopped button mushrooms
Handful of fresh coriander, finely chopped
2 tsp Turmeric,1 tsp cumin, 1 tsp chilli powder
400ml Can of coconut milk
2 tbsp Tomato purée
2 tbsp Ground almonds
Salt and pepper
1 tbsp Coconut oil

Method

1. Heat the coconut oil in a large pan, once melted add the chopped chicken breast and cook for a few minutes.
2. Add the onion, ginger and garlic and cook for a few more minutes, then throw in the chopped veg and continue to cook until the onion softens.
3. Add the coriander, turmeric, cumin, chilli powder and stir until everything is coated with the spices. Add the remaining ingredients and stir well.
4. Allow to simmer for 20 mins, serve with rice or enjoy on its own.

PASTE
RED
ONION
PUMPKIN
COURGETTE

Thai Green Curry

Ingredients:

Serves 2

2 Chicken breasts or 500g pumpkin
1 Red onion
1 x 400ml Can coconut milk
1 tbsp Coconut oil
2 tbsp Green curry paste (homemade or bought)
2 Cups of assorted veg - chopped peppers, courgette, baby corn, sugar snap peas, carrots
Pinch of salt
Brown /basmati rice or quinoa (Optional)

Method:

1. In the pan, heat the coconut oil and add the chicken (if using) and chopped onion, cook for 5 minutes.
2. Add the coconut milk, green paste and simmer for 2 minutes.
3. Add the vegetables, a pinch of salt and pumpkin (if using) and place lid on the pan, simmer for 20 minutes or until the veg is cooked.
4. Cook the rice or quinoa whilst the curry is simmering.

Thai Green Curry Paste

Ingredients to make 2 tbsp:

1 Green chilli, seeds removed if you don't like hot curries!
1 Thumb sized piece ginger
2 Garlic cloves
2 Spring onions, chopped
Juice of one lemon
Handful of fresh coriander
Handful of fresh mint
Handful of fresh basil
1 tbsp Fish sauce

Method

1. Finely chop all the ingredients and place everything in a blender with the lemon juice and fish sauce.
2. Blast until a smooth paste is formed.
3. If you don't use all of the paste you can store it in the fridge in a sealed jar for a couple of days.

Chicken Goujons

Ingredients:

Serves 2

2 Chicken breasts cut into strips
1 Egg, whisked
4 tbsp Wholemeal or gluten free flour
4 tbsp Desiccated coconut
Salt and pepper
Dried or fresh rosemary finely chopped
4 tbsp Coconut oil

Method

1. Preheat the oven to 180°C/160°C fan. Heat the coconut oil in a large frying pan on a medium heat.
2. Add the chopped rosemary to the flour with a pinch of salt and pepper and place in a bowl. In separate bowls place the desiccated coconut and in another bowl the egg.
3. Roll the chicken strips in the flour, then egg, then desiccated coconut and place in the pan.
4. Repeat with all the chicken. Colour on all sides then place on a tray lined with greaseproof paper.
5. Pop in the oven for 15 minutes or until cooked through.
6. Serve with sweet potato fries, salad and homemade mayo!

Sweet Potato Fries

Ingredients:

Serves 2

1 Large sweet potato
2 tsp Smoked paprika
Salt and pepper
Dried or fresh rosemary finely chopped
2 tbsp Coconut oil

Method

1. Heat the coconut oil in the microwave so it becomes liquid then stir in the paprika.
2. Peel, the potato then chop into strips to make the fries.
3. Place the fries in a pan of boiling water on a medium heat for 5 minutes to soften.
4. Drain the fries and leave to cool slightly, this will help them stay fluffy inside and crisp on the outside!
5. Place on a tray lined with baking paper the pour over the coconut oil mixture, sprinkle with salt, pepper and the rosemary. Then using your hands mix the potatoes with the oil and herbs until they are all evenly coated.
6. Place in the oven at 200°/180°C fan until crispy (about 30mins), you may need to turn them half way through.

Quinoa Burgers

Ingredients:

Serves 2

120 g Quinoa
200ml Boiling water
1 Red onion very finely chopped
1 Garlic clove crushed
½ Courgette
2 Eggs, whisked
1 tbsp. Coconut oil
Salt and pepper

Method:

1. Place the quinoa in a pan with the water and gently simmer for about 15 minutes or until the quinoa is fully puffed out. Remove from heat and drain if there is any water left in the pan.
2. Place the coconut oil, courgette, red onion and garlic in a frying pan and cook until onion is soft. Place cooked ingredients in a large bowl with the cooked and cooled quinoa and the eggs.
3. Using your hands combine the ingredients together and form 4-5 burgers.
4. Place in the fridge for at least one hour.
5. Heat the coconut in a large pan and add the burgers. Cook for about 4 minutes on each side until cooked right through.

Carrot Slaw

Ingredients

2 Carrots, peeled then grated
Juice of half a lemon
2 Spring onions, very finely chopped
2 tbsp Natural yoghurt or homemade mayo (p114)

Method

1. Combine all ingredients in a bowl and serve as a fresh side dish.
2. You could also try adding sliced apple, walnuts, raisins or even some of the curry powder (p112) to spice it up!

Roasted Squash and Quinoa

Ingredients:
Serves one
1 Small pumpkin or squash
½ cup Quinoa
Small handful of dried cranberries
Small handful of macadamia nuts, lightly crushed
100g Sweetcorn
2 Spring onions
Coconut oil
Serve with salad

Method:
1. Heat the oven to 180°C/160°C fan.
2. Cut the top off the pumpkin and scrape out all of the seeds.
3. Place 1 tsp of coconut oil in the pumpkin then place on a tray in the oven for 30mins. If you are in a rush, you can do this in the microwave on high for 10-15 mins.
4. Place the quinoa in a pan and cover with hot water, some salt and pepper and leave to simmer for 15-20mins until cooked.
5. In the meantime place 1 tsp coconut oil in a frying pan on a medium heat. Add the spring onions, dried cranberries and macadamia nuts and cook until onions are soft.
6. Once the quinoa is cooked, drain, then stir in the nut, cranberry and onion mixture. Remove the pumpkin from the oven and fill with quinoa mixture. Serve with salad or steamed kale.

Thai Red Curry

Ingredients
Serves 2

2 Turkey/ chicken breasts or 250g peeled king prawns
1 Large red onion
2 Cups of veg (mushrooms, courgette, red or yellow pepper, spinach)
1 400ml Can of coconut milk
2 tbsp Thai red curry paste (p107)
Handful of fresh coriander
1 tbsp Coconut oil

Method
1. Heat the coconut oil in a large pan on a medium heat. Add the diced chicken or turkey (if using) and cook until meat is white through.
2. Add the onions and keep stirring until they begin to soften.
3. Add the rest of the veg, along with the red curry paste. Stir well, coating all in the pan with the paste.
4. Pour in the coconut milk, stir and leave to simmer on a gentle heat for about 15mins, adding the chopped fresh coriander (and prawns if using) for the last 5 minutes. Check the prawns are soft and cooked through before removing from the heat.
5. Serve with rice or quinoa and garnish with more coriander.

Snacks

Sweet Potato Brownies

Ingredients

300g Sweet potatoes
60g Dried apricots, chopped
60g Medjool dates, pitted and chopped
60g Dark chocolate (80-90% cocoa)
100g Ground almonds
2 tsp Raw cacao powder
1 tsp Coconut oil

Method

1. Pre heat the oven to 180 °C/160°C fan. Peel and cube the sweet potato and place in a pan to boil until soft enough to mash. Once soft, place the sweet potato in a blender and blend until a smooth paste is formed.
2. In a non-stick pan, place the apricots, dates, dark chocolate and coconut oil, heat until the apricots become soft and the chocolate has melted.
3. Add the apricot chocolate mixture to the sweet potato and blend again.
4. Add the ground almonds and cacao powder to the blender, then blast one last time, making sure the mixture is even and there is no orange potato showing.
6. Spoon the mixture in to a lined tray and place in the oven for about 20 minutes or until you can pierce the brownie with a fork and bring it out clean. For the final 3-5mins, turn the heat up to 220°C/200°C fan to firm the top up.

Super Seed & Berry Biscuits

Ingredients:

130g Oats
50g Pumpkin seeds
25g Sunflower seeds
50g Dried cranberries
25g Goji berries
2 tbsp Honey
1 Egg
1 tbsp Good quality peanut butter (100% peanuts, no added sugar)

Method:

1. Preheat the oven to 160°C/140°C fan.
2. Mix oats, seeds and berries in a large bowl
3. Heat the honey and peanut butter slightly then pour over oat mixture. Mix thoroughly, coating everything.
4. Whisk the egg and pour over the mixture and again mix thoroughly.
5. Spoon onto a baking tray and form round biscuits. I use biscuit cutters to press the mixture into to make the shape of the biscuit when it is on the tray.
6. Bake for 20mins or until lightly golden then remove from the oven and allow to cool before storing in an air tight container.

F

Banana Loaf

Ingredients:
170g Ground almonds
1 tsp Baking powder
2 Eggs
A pinch of salt
2 tbsp Honey
2 Bananas (over ripe)
2 tbsp Coconut oil
Handful of dried apricots, finely chopped or 1/2 cup fresh or frozen raspberries

Method:
1. Preheat the oven to 170°C/150°C fan.
2. In a bowl, mix ground almonds and baking powder together.
3. In a separate bowl, whisk the eggs, honey, coconut oil and bananas.
4. Stir in the almond mixture, then apricots or raspberries.
5. Place mixture into a greased and lined loaf tin or into muffin cases.
6. Bake until golden, approximately 40-50mins if cooking a loaf, slightly less if doing muffins.

Coconut Chocolate Slice

Ingredients:
300g Mixed nuts
30g Sunflower seeds
45g Pumpkin seeds
150g Dates
2 tbsp Maple syrup
3 tbsp Coconut oil
50g Desiccated coconut
2 tbsp Raw cacao powder

Method:
1. Preheat oven to 160°C/140°C fan. Give the dates a blast in the blender then place in a pan with the coconut oil and maple syrup, gently heat until dates are sticky.
2. Place the rest of the ingredients in the blender until they form a breadcrumb consistency.
3. Add the date mixture to the blender and blast until well mixed.
4. Press into a square tin lined with greaseproof paper and cook for 45mins.
5. Cut whilst warm then lift the whole bake out of the tray using the greaseproof paper and leave to cool on a rack before separating the slices.

Coconut and Date Power Balls

Ingredients:

175g Dates
20g Desiccated coconut (plus a sprinkle for decorating)
30g Ground almonds
2 tsp Raw cacao powder
Optional- Zest of one orange
Optional - 1 tsp Orange juice

Method:

1. Blend the dates for a minute then pop them in the microwave for 1 min.
2. Place the dates back in the blender along with all the other ingredients and blast until they start to bind together.
3. Using your hands, mould the mixture into six balls then roll in some of the desiccated coconut to finish!

Grain Free Flapjack

Ingredients:

130g Hazelnuts
100g Cashew nuts
130g Dates (chopped up)
3 tbsp Coconut oil
1 tbsp Honey
50g Dried cranberries
30g Pumpkin seeds

Method:

1. Preheat oven to 170°C/150°C fan. Blend the hazelnuts and cashew nuts to form a rough mixture.
2. In a pan heat the coconut oil and honey, add the dates and stir until they become soft and 'gooey'.
3. Take off the heat and leave to cool for 5 mins.
4. Pour the date mixture into the blender and zap until it all starts to stick together and everything is combined.
5. Stir in the cranberries and pumpkin seeds then press into a tin lined with greaseproof paper.
6. Place in the oven and bake for 25mins or until it starts to colour.
7. Cut whilst warm and leave to cool before removing from the tray.

MAPLE & CINNAMON
POPCORN
& PECANS
APPLE
CRISPS

Maple & Cinnamon Popcorn

Ingredients

1 Cup of popcorn kernels
2 tbsp Maple syrup
2 tsp Cinnamon
2 tsp Coconut oil

Method

1. In a large pan, melt the coconut oil.
2. Once melted, add the popcorn kernels and place a lid on the pan.
3. Listen for the corn popping and once there a very few pops, remove from the heat.
4. Pour the syrup over the popcorn whilst it is still warm then sprinkle the cinnamon over the top.
5. Mix thoroughly so the popcorn is well coated.
6. The popcorn will be quite sticky so place in the oven on the lowest heat or in a dehydrator for a couple of hours to dry it out. Store in an air tight container or bag and eat within a couple of days.

Apple Crisps

Ingredients

2 Apples, very thinly sliced into discs

Method

1. Place the thinly sliced apple on a baking tray lined with paper and place in the oven on the lowest heat for a few hours.
2. You will be able to tell when they are done as the will feel dry and a little chewy, they will not go crispy but still make handy little snacks. If you have access to a dehydrator, then you could use this instead.

Cinnamon Toasted Pecans

Ingredients

100g Pecan nuts
2 tsp Coconut oil
1 tsp Cinnamon
2 tsp Maple syrup

Method

1. Preheat the oven to 180°C/160°C fan. Place the maple syrup and coconut oil in a dish and microwave until the coconut oil is runny, stir in the cinnamon.
2. Place the pecan nuts in a bowl then pour the maple syrup mixture over the nuts.
3. Mix well so the nuts are well coated. Place on a tray lined with baking parchment and pop in the oven.
4. Check after 5 minutes then pop back in the oven if the nuts aren't starting to colour. Watch carefully as they soon cook!

Savoury Crackers

Ingredients:

150g Hazelnuts
75g Almonds
50g Ground flax
25g Pumpkin seeds
1 Egg
2 tbsp Water
Sesame seeds for decoration

Method

1. Preheat oven to 180°C/160°C fan and line two baking trays with greaseproof paper.
2. Place all the nuts and seeds (apart from the sesame seeds) in the blender and finely grind them.
3. Remove from the blender and add the egg and water, stir well so the mixture is fully combined.
4. Divide the dough into two balls and place each one in the centre of one of your lined trays.
5. Place another piece of greaseproof paper over the dough then roll it out using a rolling pin to about 3mm thick.
6. Cut the dough into squares or rectangles using a knife but without moving the crackers apart.
7. Sprinkle with sesame seeds then place in the oven for 10 to 15 minutes.
8. Remove from the oven and allow to cool. Separate the biscuits then store in an air tight container for 3-5days.

These little crackers are fab for on the go, great for dipping in hummus, guacamole or even soups. They are packed with protein so can make great little post work out snacks and also a great cracker alternative on a cheese board if you are having a dinner party!

Hummus

Ingredients

1 400g can Chickpeas, drained

Juice ½ a lemon (more if you like your hummus tangy!)

1 Clove of garlic

Salt

Water

2 tbsp Olive oil

2 tbsp Tahini

Method

1. Blend all ingredients together adding a little water at a time until it reaches the texture you like.
2. Add a little salt and some more lemon juice to taste.
3. To add extra flavour to your hummus, try adding a teaspoon of pesto (p114) or blending in some roasted red peppers.

Guacamole

Ingredients

1 Avocado
1/2 Red onion
Juice of one lime
Handful of fresh coriander
5 Cherry tomatoes
1 tbsp olive oil
1 Chilli (optional)
Salt and pepper

Method

1. Finely chop the onions, tomato, chilli (if using) and coriander.
2. Mash the avocado in a bowl using a fork, combine with the other ingredients above.
3. Squeeze in the lime juice, add a drizzle of olive oil and give a good grind of salt and pepper, stir and serve!

Curried Popcorn

Ingredients

1 Cup of popcorn kernels

1 tbsp Curry powder (p112) or a mixture of turmeric, cumin and chilli powder

2 tsp Coconut oil

Method

1. In a large pan, melt the coconut oil.
2. Once melted, add the popcorn kernels and place a lid on the pan.
3. Listen for the corn popping and once there a very few pops, remove from the heat.
4. Allow to cool a little before sprinkling over the curry powder and mixing well.
5. Store in an air tight jar or bag for up to a week.

Crispy Kale

Ingredients

100g Kale

1 tsp Olive oil

Salt

Method

1. Preheat the oven to 160°C/140°C fan.
2. Line a baking tray with parchment.
3. Remove the stems from the kale, rinse and pat dry.
4. Place the kale on the tray, drizzle with olive oil and sprinkle with a little salt.
5. Place in the oven for 10 minutes then turn the kale and place back in the oven for a further 5 minutes.
6. Once they start to crisp up, remove from the oven and allow to cool, if you give them a few minutes to cool before trying them they should crisp up even more!

CURRY
POWDER
POPCORN
SNACKS
CRISPY
KALE

Side Dishes And Spices

Colourful Roasties

Ingredients:

1/2 Butternut squash
3 Beetroot
2 tbsp Coconut oil
2 Springs of fresh rosemary
Sea salt

Method

1. Preheat the oven to 180°C/160°C fan.
2. Cube the squash and the beetroot.
3. Place on one baking tray the squash and another the beetroot, drizzle with melted coconut oil and sprinkle over the rosemary and a good grind of sea salt.
4. Pop in the oven for about 30 mins or until both are soft.

Cauliflower Mash

Ingredients

1 Cauliflower head
1 tbsp Crème fraiche
Salt and pepper

Method

1. Separate the florets of cauliflower then place in a pan of boiling water.
2. Simmer until soft.
3. Place in a blender with the crème fraise and a good grind of salt and pepper.
4. Blend until a smooth creamy mash is formed with no lumps in, season to taste.

Thai Red Curry Paste

Ingredients

1 or 2 Red chillies (depending on how hot you like your curry!)
2 tsp Coriander seeds
2 tsp Cumin seeds
1 Thumb sized piece of ginger
2 Shallots or one small red onion
Juice of one lemon
Juice of one lime
1 tbsp Hot paprika

Method

1. Heat the seeds in a dry frying pan on a high heat for a couple of minutes before crushing the seeds using a pestle and mortar to form a powder.
2. Finely chop the other ingredients and place them in the blender with the powder then blast until a paste is formed.
3. Store in a clean jar in the fridge for up to a couple of days if you are not using immediately.

Curry Powder Mix

Ingredients

1 tbsp Turmeric
2 tbsp Ground coriander
1 tbsp Ground cumin
1 tsp Chilli powder

Method

1.Mix all the spices together and store in a sealed jar, use in a selection of dishes including my fragrant curries.

Moroccan Spice Mix

Ingredients

1 tsp Allspice
1 tsp Cayenne
1 tsp Ground cinnamon
1 tsp Salt
1 tsp Black pepper
2 tsp Ground ginger
2 tsp Ground cumin

Method

1. Mix all the spices together and store in a sealed jar, use to spice up fish or chicken.

Pesto

Ingredients

1 Garlic clove
Large handful of basil leaves
2 tbsp Pine nuts or Brazil nuts or walnuts
Juice of one lemon
2 tbsp Grated parmesan (optional)
1 tbsp Olive oil (unless using the pesto for chicken Kiev's, no oil needed)

Method

1. Finely chop the basil leaves and grind in a pestle and mortar with the other ingredients until a paste is formed to your desired consistency or place all in a blender to form the paste.
2. Use with fish, veg, pasta, chicken or add a dollop to your hummus for extra flavour!
3. Store in a sealed jar in the fridge for up to a couple of days if not using immediately.

Cajun Spice Mix

Ingredients

1 tsp Garlic Powder
2 tsp Paprika
1 tsp Oregano
1 tsp Thyme
1 tsp Cayenne pepper
1 tsp Chilli (optional)

Method

1.Mix all the spices together and store in a sealed jar to use with meat, fish or veg.

Homemade Mayo

Ingredients

2 Egg yolks
150ml olive oil
Juice of one lemon
1 heaped tsp Dijon mustard

Method

1. Place the egg yolks, lemon juice and mustard in a jug, using a hand blender mix them well.
2. Keep the hand blender on and slowly add the olive oil, drizzling a little at a time until the mixture forms a mayonnaise consistency.
3. Store in a clean jar in the fridge for up to 3 days.

Meal Plans

4 Weeks of Meal Plans

On the next few pages are four weeks of meal plans, they contain a variety of meals and snacks that should help you on your way to a cleaner mind set about your daily eating habits.
If you don't want to do these exact meal plans, use them as examples for planning out your own. I recommend sitting down on a one night a week and planning out your week so you don't stray from your plan, this also helps when you go shopping, if you know what you need to get then you won't buy anything that will be wasted (also saving you some money) and you won't head to the naughty aisles!

Each meal is designed to fill you up, with little snacks in between to keep your energy levels steady, your metabolism burning and fill the gaps. Try and leave a couple of hours between every meal or snack, this allows your body to digest the food properly.

Stick your meal plan on the fridge or somewhere that you can see it to help you keep on track!

Week One

Day	Breakfast	Snack	Lunch	Snack	Dinner
1	Feta eggs	Handful of toasted pecans	Super greens soup & savoury crackers	2 Hardboiled eggs	Quinoa burgers & veg
2	Porridge & berries	Grainfree flapjack	Pastry free quiche & salad	2 Savoury crackers & 1tbsp hummus	Thai red curry
3	Homemade granola & berries	Handful of toasted pecans	Curried quinoa	1 Apple & 1tbsp nut butter	Turkey mince bolognaise & salad
4	2 Poached Eggs & One slice of rye toast	Grainfree flapjack	Pastry free quiche & salad	2 Savoury crackers & 1 tbsp hummus	Pesto veg & fish
5	2 Dippy eggs & asparagus	4 tbsp Greek yoghurt & 1/2 cup of berries	Super greens soup & savoury crackers	Grainfree flapjack	Lentil & bean casserole
6	Porridge & berries	1 Apple & 1 tsp nut butter	Left over lentil & bean casserole	1 Hardboiled egg & 1 carrot in sticks	Prawn stir fry
7	Bacon fritters	4 tbsp Greek yoghurt & 1/2 cup of berries	Rosemary & lemon chicken, veg & colourful roasties	-	Thai pumpkin soup & 2 savoury crackers with 2 tbsp cottage cheese

If you feel you need something sweet after your night time meal, try having some dark choc, two pieces the size of a £1 coin. Or have some natural / Greek yoghurt (about 3 tbsp).

Week Two

Day	Breakfast	Snack	Lunch	Snack	Dinner
1	Berry omelette	Handful of toasted pecans	Chicken & hummus salad & 1 apple	1 Date power ball	Chilli
2	2 Poached eggs & 1 slice of rye toast	Mixed nuts	Thai pumpkin soup & 2 slices of halloumi	4 tbsp Yoghurt & ½ cup berries	Buckwheat risotto
3	Salmon, eggy avocado & spinach	1 Date power ball	Pesto chicken salad	1 Apple & 1tbsp nut butter	Thai green curry
4	Porridge & berries	40g Mixed nuts	Goats cheese & peas on toast	1 Hard boiled egg & carrot sticks	Chicken & chickpea casserole
5	2 Dippy eggs & asparagus	4 tbsp Greek yoghurt & ½ cup of berries	Mixed bean salad	1 Date power ball	Roasted squash & quinoa
6	2 Scrambled eggs & 1 slice of rye toast	Handful toasted pecans	Kale & halloumi salad & 1 apple	4 tbsp Yoghurt & ½ cup berries	Salmon frittata
7	Homemade granola & 4 tbsp Greek yoghurt	40g mixed nuts	Lamb chops & veg	-	Tomato soup & 3 savoury crackers with 2 tbsp cottage cheese

If you don't have time to make the rye bread, you can find it in health food stores and many bigger supermarkets. If you don't enjoy rye bread then look for wholegrain bread, just plain brown bread is a less healthy option.

Week Three

Day	Breakfast	Snack	Lunch	Snack	Dinner
1	2 Scrambled eggs & 30g smoked salmon	4 tbsp Greek yoghurt & 1/2 cup of berries	Pesto frittata	1 Square sweet potato brownie	Chicken Goujons, sweet potato fries & salad
2	Homemade granola & 4 tbsp Greek yoghurt	2 oat cakes with 1tbsp nut butter	Tomato soup & 3 savoury crackers & 1 apple	2 Hard boiled eggs	Chicken korma
3	Sweet potato hash brown, poached egg & salmon	1 Apple	Halloumi, peppers & pine nuts	1 Square sweet potato brownie	Pesto chicken & courgetti
4	Porridge & berries	40g Mixed nuts	Moroccan chicken salad	Guacamole & 2 savoury crackers	Cajun spiced salmon
5	Salmon, eggy avocado & spinach	1 Pear	Curried quinoa	1 Square sweet potato brownie	Meatballs & courgetti
6	2 Poached eggs & 1 slice of rye toast	Handful toasted pecans	Goats cheese & roasted peppers	4 tbsp Yoghurt & 1/2 cup berries	Stir fry veg & smoked haddock
7	Chocolate hazelnut pancakes	40g mixed nuts	Carrot & coriander soup with 3 savoury crackers	4 tbsp Yoghurt & 1/2 cup berries	Lasagne & salad

When you're buying nut butters, make sure they contain only nuts, as many contain loads of sugar and oils. Why not try almond or cashew nut butter instead of peanut butter to mix it up a bit!

Week Four

Day	Breakfast	Snack	Lunch	Snack	Dinner
1	2 Dippy eggs & asparagus	4 tbsp Greek yoghurt & 1/2 cup of berries	Salmon & pomegranate salad	Coconut chocolate slice	Lamb stew & veg
2	2 Poached eggs & 1 slice of rye toast	40g Mixed nuts	Carrot & coriander soup & 2 slices of halloumi	4 tbsp Yoghurt & 1/2 cup berries	Chicken Kiev & veg
3	Porridge & berries	1 Hard boiled egg	Pesto prawn salad	Coconut chocolate slice	Fish curry
4	2 Scrambled eggs on one slice of rye toast	1 Apple	Ham & cottage cheese wrap	Kale crisps & carrot sticks	Salmon with Thai green veg
5	Granola & 4tbsp Greek yoghurt	Coconut chocolate slice	Courgette & spinach soup with 2 hard boiled eggs	40g Mixed nuts	Chicken & chickpea casserole
6	2 Scrambled eggs & 1 slice of rye toast	Handful toasted pecans	Chicken breast with carrot slaw & salad	4 tbsp Yoghurt & 1/2 cup berries	Salmon frittata
7	Banana pancakes	40g mixed nuts	Courgette & spinach soup with 3 savoury crackers with cottage cheese	Coconut chocolate slice	Lentil & Bean Casserole

If you don't get chance to make the savoury crackers, you can always use rye crackers instead, just make sure they don't contain any added rubbish, the fewer ingredients the better!

Index of Recipes

Index of Recipes...continued

Time and care has been taken to put these recipes and meal plans together but the author can accept no responsibility for any claims that may arise from the misuse of this book. The advice and ideas in this book are intended as a general guide and do not replace the advice of healthcare professionals; if you have and health conditions, you should seek advice from a health care professional. The author disclaims any responsibility for any conditions or illness that occurs as a direct or indirect result of using this book.

A special thanks to Caroline Whalley who has helped me put this book together
X